Good enough

THE UNDERACHIEVER'S MANIFESTO

Other books by the author

THE UNDERACHIEV-ER'S MANIFESTO

The Guide to Accomplishing Little and Feeling Great

Ray Bennett, M.D.

CHRONICLE BOOKS
SAN FRANCISCO

Library of Congress Cataloging-in-Publication
Data available.

ISBN-10: 0-8118-5368-3
ISBN-13: 978-0-8118-5368-2

Manufactured in China.

Designed by Ayako Akazawa
Typesetting by Janis Reed

10 9 8 7 6 5 4 3 2

Chronicle Books LLC
680 Second Street
San Francisco, California 94107

www.chroniclebooks.com

FOR J. T.

WITHOUT HIS DEDICA-
TION TO MEDIOCRITY,
THIS BOOK WOULD NOT
HAVE BEEN POSSIBLE.

At no time in the world will a man who is sane

Over-reach himself,

Over-spend himself,

Over-rate himself.

—Lao Tzu

All is vanity. What do people gain from all

the toil at which they toil under the sun?

—Ecclesiastes 1:2–3

Sell not yourself at little price,

being so precious in God's eyes.

—Rumi

CONTENTS

INTRODUCTION

Congratulations! Opening this book is the best decision you've ever made. There, that was easy, wasn't it?

The pleasures of underachievement are many, but they are all too often lost in the pressure for success. (Or, SUCCESS!) The achievement lobby is powerful, and underachievement is, surprisingly, not as easy as it should be. Our world is so full of unrelenting messages about being the best you can be that it may not have even occurred to you to try for anything less. We've been brainwashed over many years to believe that striving for success is essential to our well-being. *Be number one! Don't settle for second best! Give 110 percent!* It's an endless, exhausting litany, thanks to advertising stars and corporate executives busy cashing in our inadequacies for their overpriced sneakers and shiny BMWs. Never mind that no one agrees on what it means to be "the best," and that it's actually impossible for *everyone* to be it, whatever it is. Maybe you're working really hard at resisting all that, but even if you are, chances are you're still striving in some way to live life to the very best—and it's killing you.

Consider: How many brilliant careers are coupled with disastrous marriages? How many talented, hardworking people smoke too much, exercise too little, or drink themselves into oblivion each week? At the other extreme, how many fitness-crazed or hypercompetitive individuals tear up their knees running marathons or risk life and limb scrambling to mountain-tops? How many brilliant and ambitious people dream of winning accolades for their genius, only to wind up working for their C+ colleagues? And even if you do manage to just about maintain a full-sprint schedule of personal and professional achievement, it can take something as common-place as the flu to throw your whole highly tuned enterprise stressfully out of whack. What you've never realized all these years is that it's your commitment to excellence that is the source of your trouble. And that's where this book can help.

In these pages you'll learn how to live life to the minimum and love it. If that sounds like a strategy to maximize happiness . . . okay, it is. But that is the exception that proves the rule. When you picked up this book, maybe you were feeling a little guilty about your halfhearted effort at work; or perhaps you've given up on an exercise regimen because you just can't pound the pavement like you did in high school. You feel like you should be doing more, or doing something better, or, more likely, doing it *all* better. But you'll soon get over that and enjoy the contentment that results from giving less than your very best. It's all about the right balance, the right amount of effort, which is probably a lot less than you've been led to believe. In our overachieving society, a little underachievement is the necessary corrective.

So relax, read this book, and put your potential back in the lockbox. Turn everything down a notch. Lower the bar. Discover the laziness that has so far eluded you. No matter who you are, there's something you're trying too hard at.

PART 1

THE BASICS

ACHIEVEMENT: THE DANGEROUS ADDICTION

Despite everything you may have heard about striving for excellence, mediocrity is the key to happiness. Consider: There are more than six billion people on the planet. Almost none of them care about your latest victory in the stock market, or the promotion you "earned." You finally bought that new car? Found a way to swing the payments on a bigger house? You lost six pounds last week? Wonderful. A disconcerting number of the six billion are just trying to get enough food to stay alive.

But also consider: They don't care if you fell flat on your face, either. They don't care if you're ugly, lazy, or out of shape. It doesn't matter to them if Suzy Perfect scored thirty points higher than you on the last math test, or if you were cut from the football team. You didn't meet your sales quota, lost your job, and feel humiliated? Take heart; the world won't hold it against you. It's a simple fact of life that your successes and failures really don't matter to nearly everybody alive. And the sooner you realize that, the sooner you can take comfort from it and get on with underachievement. Think globally; underachieve locally.

On the home front, too, achievement isn't all it's cracked up to be. Your friends, colleagues, and neighbors—and even your own family—may be less thrilled with your stellar accomplishments than you think. They may not show it, and no doubt some of them are even

adept at sounding sincerely pleased about your success, but have no illusions. They have been taught that striving for excellence is the key to *their* happiness as well. If there are winners, there are also losers, so if you're "winning," what does that mean they're doing? Must you cast your friends and loved ones in such comparative shade? The truth is, if you had any notions of making people admire you by accomplishing great things in life, forget it. You're doing more harm than good. Let us all join hands and do less together. Then maybe let's all take a nap.

Now you might protest: "But I'm not out to feel superior. I just want to make a ton of money." Or maybe, "I really *do* want perfect abs and buns of steel." There's nothing intrinsically wrong with those sentiments, except that your assessment of these goals is relative. Studies have shown that people's sense of satisfaction in life is so closely tied to their standing in relation to those around them that even absolute gains don't make them happy. Want to feel great about your income? Move to the third world. You climbed Mount Rainier? That's great . . . until you find out that your neighbor climbed Mount Everest. Got a raise? It feels great until you discover that your colleague got one, too. It actually feels like an insult if her raise is a little higher. Constant comparison with people who are smarter, more successful, and more beautiful than we are breeds frustration and jealousy. Striving is suffering.

So why do we do it?

From an early age, we've all been taught that achievement is our friend. There was a lot

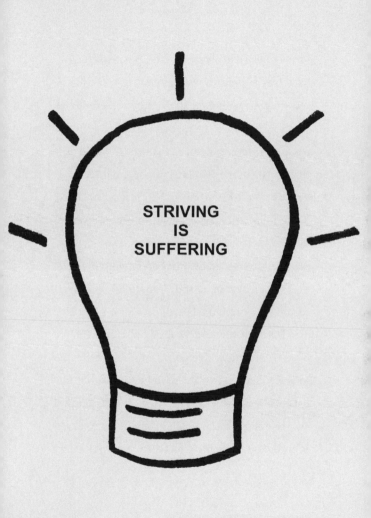

for us to learn growing up, and positive feed-back was a great way to motivate us. Teachers rewarded us with gold stars and good grades when we did well. And when we didn't do well, negative feedback helped us along, too. Didn't turn in the homework assignment? No recess. This applied to a lot more than just schoolwork. Athletic, artistic, and social achievement were always rewarded in so many ways, and in the process, we learned how to become fit, educated, occasionally creative, and (hopefully) socially responsible individuals.

But then there's everybody else. You can be a hypercompetitive golfer who maintains the lowest handicap in your social network, but just because you shot a seventy-two on your home course doesn't mean you'll be challenging Tiger Woods. You probably won't even earn a dime for the showing, and if you stop to think about it, all you've done is piss off your buddies who all wish *they* could have had the low score. Ditto for your social network, where if you spend enormous effort to impress your "friends" just so you'll fit in, odds are you could use some better, *truer* friends.

If you are like most people, however, this realization comes slowly, if at all. We're so brainwashed into believing that achievement is essential that we don't even question the idea. Even if we're resigned to being mediocre in one or more parts of our lives, we usually try to find some way to feel superior to others. And while there's nothing wrong with trying to be better at some component of our lives, for many people achievement becomes more than a goal. It becomes an *addiction*.

Some people who make more than half a million dollars a year will spend vast amounts of intellectual energy trying to cheat the tax code and squeeze out another ten grand. Amateur athletes will devote enormous amounts of time in training, at the expense of their personal relationships. Otherwise mild-mannered individuals can become rabid with piety as they outmaneuver one another for prominence in their churches. And for all its victims, the addiction of achievement leaves behind failed relationships, unhealthy bodies, corrupted minds, or some terrible combination of all three. It's a sickness that would be considered an epidemic, but of course too many doctors are afflicted with the disease to recognize the symptoms.

The key is to retrain your mind and soul, to develop healthy attitudes to ensure that you'll never fall into the trap of high-intensity, strive-for-success-at-all-costs thinking. It's not easy, but if you take to heart the core principles and attitudes outlined here, you'll be well on your way to a happier existence. Will you be less productive? That will depend on whom you ask, but if there isn't at least one important person in your life who thinks you're living below your potential, then you've got work to do.

THE TEN PRINCIPLES OF UNDERACHIEVEMENT

Before we move on to specifics, it's important to lay out the ten principles that form the foundation of underachievement. As you've probably gathered from the great, groaning shelves of self-help books out there, any book that purports to offer guidance must include numbered lists: seven habits, twenty-nine leadership secrets, one thousand inspiring ideas. Here are ten. Not too bad. Not great, but not bad.

1. Life's too short.

2. Control is an illusion.

3. Expectations lead to misery.

4. Great expectations lead to great misery.

5. Achievement creates expectations.

6. The law of diminishing returns applies everywhere.
7. Perfect is the enemy of good.
8. The tallest blade of grass is the surest to be cut.
9. Accomplishment is in the eye of the beholder.
10. The 4 Percent Value-Added Principle.

Here's a closer look at each of these principles.

1. Life's too short. It's no surprise that most of us live our lives without paying homage to the grim reaper. Death can be a frightening prospect, but it's not like you can avoid it. After all, no one ever got out of this world alive. An estimated 100 billion people have lived and died to date. That's astonishing, isn't it? Of the six-billion-plus people on the planet right now, every last one of them is going to be dead someday, and in geologic time, that someday is less than a second away. You can drive yourself into a frenzy trying to do as much as you can while you're here, or you can relax and enjoy your split second. It's your choice.

2. Control is an illusion. None of us is in total control of our lives, and if you think you are, then count your blessings: that's a delightful illusion. But then again, it can be pretty liberating after you screw up something really important to sit back, relax, and say, "It wasn't my fault . . . it was out of my control."

Consider this interesting fact: In 1998, a group of business students from the University of Washington asked two of the richest men in the world, Bill Gates and Warren Buffet, what they felt was the biggest single factor in their success. Their reply? Being born and living in America. They didn't have any control over either. It's a lot like saying that the best way to succeed in life is to choose your parents well. You didn't choose them, or your genes, or a multitude of other factors that have had an enormous impact on your life. So why put all that pressure on yourself to succeed just because you were given a great mind or superb physical talent? And if you don't have those things, well . . . it wasn't your fault in the first place.

3. *Expectations lead to misery.* Surely you can remember a day when you started with a plan firmly in mind, only to let some minor

CONTROL
IS AN
ILLUSION

annoyance (the weather, a missed bus, a hang-nail) get the better of you. The tighter the script and the higher the stakes, the more likely it is that something won't go as planned. It's no accident that the most common and most important piece of advice to keep in mind when planning a wedding is to treat the actual event more like a party than a play. The most bitter A scored on a chemistry test is the one on which you were sure you'd gotten an A+. Maybe you were hoping to lose ten pounds in two weeks, but when you lost only five you gave up on your diet, hopeless after your "failed" effort. It would be nice to believe that setting the bar high always helps, but it doesn't. Most people start on an exercise program looking for great improvement, only to quit out of disappointment. If only they had learned to avoid expectations . . .

4. Great expectations lead to great misery. This may seem self-evident, but without it, there would have been only nine principles.

5. Achievement creates expectations. Companies that exceed their earning projections routinely raise their goals. If they fail to meet these new goals—or in some cases, if they don't exceed the new goals by enough—they stand to see their stock value hammered by miffed investors. To some, what follows is a temptation to cook the books. Welcome to Enron.

6. The law of diminishing returns applies everywhere. At some point, you really *can't* live any better, no matter *how* much money you earn—or spend. Of course, most of us don't feel we have anywhere near enough money to rest easy, and we'd like to have more to test this theory out. But if you have a swimming pool and a tennis court, will you really be as keenly excited when you buy a pool table? After you've enjoyed the view from a spectacular penthouse for a while, it gets old. The view from the new, taller, more expensive building across town may be "better," but how much better? The ten-dollar bottle of wine may taste perfectly good until you've had the hundred-dollar bottle, but is the latter bottle really ten times as good? How about the thousand-dollar bottle: a hundred times as good? Maybe it is, but does that mean you retroactively didn't enjoy the less expensive wine? Are you significantly healthier running six miles rather than "just" three? Benefits don't continue to accrue at the same rate as effort or investment. At some point, in almost any endeavor, the curve flattens out, and it may even start to dip. If you're lucky enough to be on vacation in the first place, visiting ten temples in a day is likely to erase your memory of the first six; stopping in front of 200 paintings in the Louvre is a recipe for forgetting the first 150. More is not always better, and good enough is good enough.

7. Perfect is the enemy of good. The word *perfect* shouldn't even be in the underachiever's vocabulary. To seek perfection is to be cursed to find fault in the perfectly adequate, enjoyable, or even just plain good. The dictionary paints a grim portrait of the perfectionist: a fusspot, a nitpicker, a pedant, demanding, fastidious, obsessive, punctilious, exacting. How'd you like to be married to that? Perfection is subjective,

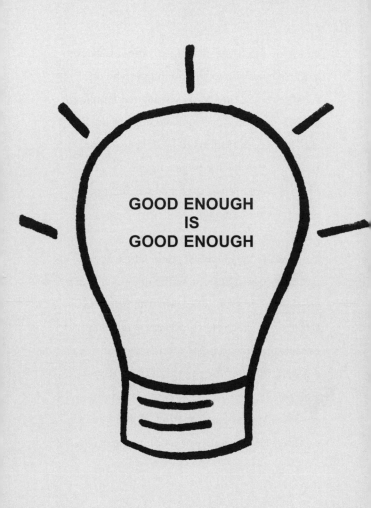

and impossible, and yet its pursuit is the driving mania of the overachiever. With perfection in mind, it's frighteningly easy and almost inevitable to push things past good to the neurotically overworked, the belabored, and the endlessly second-guessed. If something is worth doing at all, sometimes it's worth doing it half-assed.

8. The tallest blade of grass is the surest to be cut. This is also known as "flying under the radar." Many people make the mistake of thinking that accomplishment is the source of admiration, when in reality it is the source of envy and resentment. Japanese folk wisdom spells this out in more colorfully violent terms: "The nail that sticks up gets hammered down." If you're better than everyone else, you had better make sure that they don't recognize it.

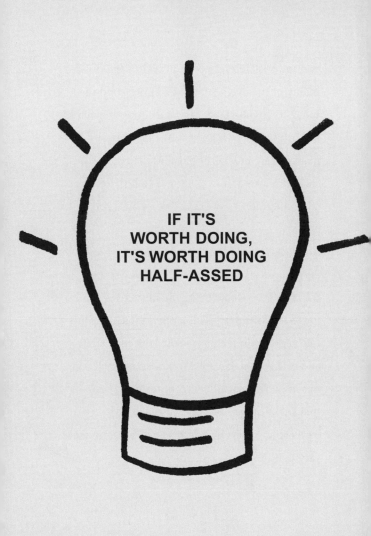

9. Accomplishment is in the eye of the beholder.
There's nothing more satisfying than seeing
some arrogant jerk boast about his accomplishments in some activity about which his audience
neither knows nor cares a whit. Ask yourself,
Who really cares?

10. The 4 Percent Value-Added Principle. It
is now an established scientific fact that human
beings are, genetically speaking, 96 percent
identical to chimpanzees. How does that make
you feel? Think of it: the most successful individuals in the world, as well as the most hopelessly underaccomplished ones, are, biologically
speaking, all pretty close to apes. If anything
puts the lie to the old saw about giving 110 percent, this is it. In fact, biologically speaking, even
bacteria are extremely "successful," and they

don't seem to work that hard at it. This point may be a case of science misapplied, but it seems to fit. Being alive at all is by far your greatest achievement.

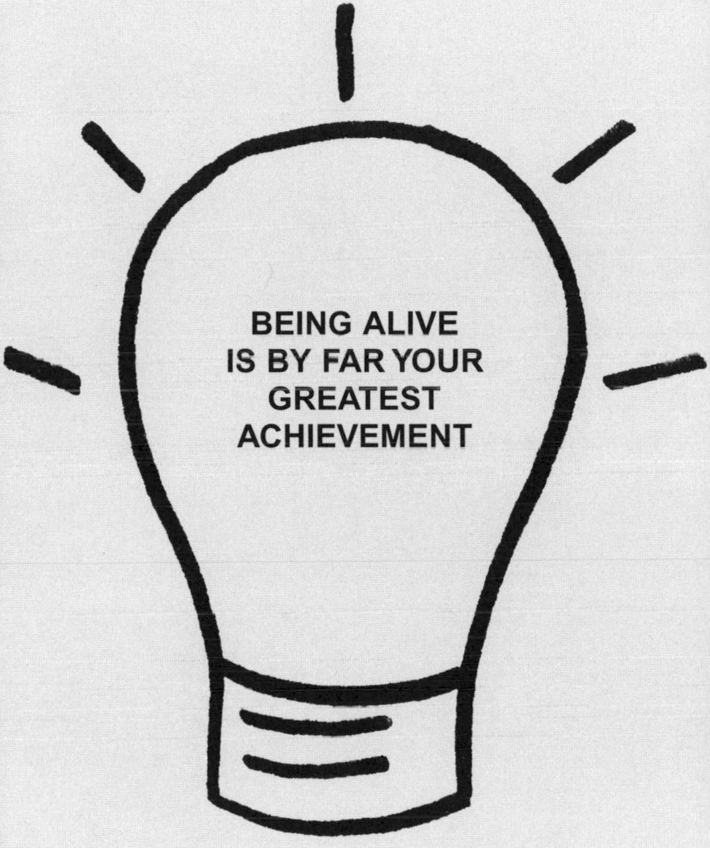
BEING ALIVE
IS BY FAR YOUR
GREATEST
ACHIEVEMENT

PART 2

APPLICATIONS: THE UNDERACHIEV-ER'S GUIDE TO LIFE

THE UNDERACHIEVER
AT WORK

Underachievers are the best, most dependable
workers. This may seem counterintuitive, but
the key here is that while *some* achievement is
necessary and good for productivity, *a lot* of it is
dangerous to you and everyone around you.
And if you have a wide enough perspective,
you'll see it's also an exercise in futility.

We've established the envy and disdain that
coworkers have for anyone who appears to be
very successful. That's human nature. Now let's
misapply some principles of physics, just for fun.
One of the fundamental laws of physics holds
that systems tend toward equilibrium. Apply this
law to the workplace and you'll see that corporate

systems exist for a variety of reasons, and one of them is to keep overachievers from making everyone else look bad while assuring a stable norm. To take a thermodynamic perspective, even the brightest, hottest-burning star cools to the temperature of its surroundings. Really, all you need is to have a bit of empathy here. Imagine how you would feel if you were consistently out-performed at work by some know-it-all. Not only would it hurt your pride, but pretty soon you'd start to worry about the security of your job. Why inflict that kind of suffering on anyone else?

One of the more toxic effects of great accomplishment is the unseemly eagerness with which people scramble to take credit for at least a part of it, especially when they feel compelled to in the pressurized atmosphere of overachieve-ment. Another is the adversarial position the overachiever must then adopt toward coworkers to either defend his turf or share the credit but feel robbed. In either case, the result is bitterness and frustration.

Underachievers aren't threatening to others. They're unlikely to screw up as often as someone pushing for perfection. If they fail at a project, oh well; no one expected much anyway. If they succeed, it will seem, paradoxically, like a fantastic achievement.

When faced with a ridiculous task to perform in an unreasonable amount of time (as happens routinely at work), the perfectionist (the pedant, the nitpicker) grumbles about the lack of resources, support, and time to complete the job perfectly. This never goes over well with one's superiors. The underachiever, free of the shackles of excellence, can step in and save the day. Odds are, the bosses will appreciate just seeing the work done without a lot of complaining. The underachiever will also find, ironically, that she is able to accomplish so much more than those who consistently strive for perfection. Work twice as hard, burn out twice as fast. Going the extra mile only leads to exhaustion.

Speaking of miles, simply getting to work can be complicated by overachievement. A study presented at the 2005 International Symposium on Transportation and Traffic showed that weaving in traffic to find the fastest lane actually makes traffic jams worse. Going with the flow keeps the commute smoother and safer.

Underachievement at work is not, however, simply about staying employed. It is also about keeping the other relationships in your life healthy. For example, if you're going to spend

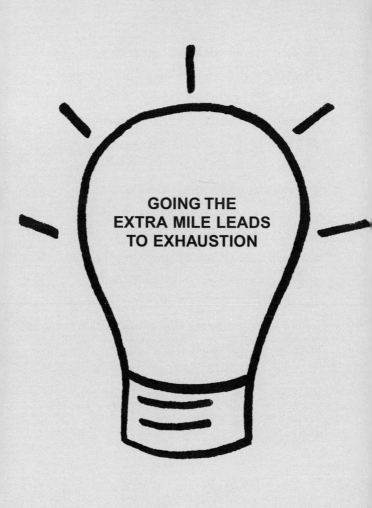

weekends at work all the time, you'd better be making wheelbarrows full of money to compensate for all the time you're not spending with your friends and family. Face the facts: you're probably not going to be a millionaire, so why kill yourself? Go home and spend a lazy weekend with your kids.

A fundamental problem faced by over-achievers is that they expect their successes to continue at the pace to which they've grown accustomed. The law of diminishing returns assures that they won't. As they move up the ladder, they will be surrounded by more successful people, it will become harder for them to stand out, and they will have to redouble their efforts. At that point, they can keep on pushing at the expense of their health and relationships, or they can dedicate themselves to becoming underachievers. We know which choice will be more healthy and productive in the long run. It's no coincidence that across many cultures we find versions of the proverb "Slow and steady wins the race." (The life span of a hare: three to four years. The life span of a tortoise: up to a hundred years.) Plus, with all the time saved by not working, underachievers can take up hobbies that will make them far more interesting to their friends. And they'll have time to spend with their friends. So they'll be able to keep their friends. After a few weeks of responses like "I'd love to, but I have an important project to finish. Call me next week," you'll find your friends won't bother calling anymore.

THE UNDERACHIEVER
IN LOVE

In today's world of instant gratification and
ubiquitous entertainment, relationships have
become a challenge. It's easier than ever to
walk away from a relationship and find other
diversions. Conversation has become a lost art,
and with the limited amount of time people
have left after working and working out, dates
often can feel like high-pressure interviews. And
so they sometimes are, literally, with the grim
overachiever invention of speed-dating.
Overexposure of celebrity relationships gives the
impression that only good-looking people have
sex. All of this creates a culture of striving in the
world of romance. Young professionals now

attack their social lives with the zeal and strategic thinking typically reserved for business planning. They are convinced that with relentless effort, the perfect mate can be found.

Underachievers recognize the folly in all of this. First, they know that ugly people have good sex, too. Of our friends and neighbors—in fact, of the six billion people on the planet—it's a common fact that very, very few of their parents were supermodels. Second, it is foolish to believe that there is only one perfect person in the world that you are supposed to meet. If you accept this terrifying and deeply depressing notion, you must also accept that you have better odds—much, much, better odds—of winning the longest-odds lottery than finding Him or Her. When you surrender the neurotic (and weirdly competitive) drive to seek only the *best* relationship, you can ease into having a pretty good one, which in life is about as good as it gets.

Playing hard-to-get is a popular sport, but that takes too much work. Trying too hard is usually a sign of desperation. In the under-achiever's relationship, a mutual respect develops as each person goes about his or her business without extreme dependence on the other. And if things don't work out, the breakup can be handled so much more easily. But odds are that if you're not constantly looking around for the fantasy you construct in your mind, you'll be more content with the real relationship you have. Once in a relationship, underachievers rec-ognize that demanding perfection in a partner is a lot like living next to a mental hospital: it's a short walk to insanity. Turn the tables here. Do

you want to be expected to be perfect? No. No, you don't.

Remember, achievement creates expectations. It's a safe bet that if you go all out and spend lavishly on your lover's birthday, the same will be expected the following year. If you don't pony up the big bucks again, you'll have some explaining to do, and it won't be pretty. It's probably also a bad idea to be in a relationship with someone who expects you to keep upping the ante.

THE UNDERACHIEVER'S DIET

Meat was bad. Then meat was good. Carbs were bad. Now carbs are okay (or they're still bad). Margarine was healthier than butter because it has less saturated fat. But margarine's fat is *trans* fat, which is bad. Sugar is bad, but it tastes good.

The underachiever feels vindicated as the deck of the Good Ship Diet Trend pitches to and fro. By staying right in the middle and not running to or from the next new dietary craze, the underachiever is always ahead of the pack when the trend eventually tips the other way. And think of all the money saved on unproven dietary supplements or expensive proprietary diet-plan foods. Why pay five times as much for a diet chocolate bar than for the chocolate bar you're actually craving?

Staying with a weight-loss program is almost impossible for anyone who goes to extremes in cutting calories. The underachiever knows that occasional cheating makes it possible to eat less overall without feeling totally deprived. The forbidden fruit (or doughnut) is always the sweetest. What distinguishes the underachieving dieter is his complete lack of guilt at consuming the occasional doughnut. A snack is only a failure if you measure success by the stress-inducing standard of total deprivation.

Consuming in moderation has always been a good idea, and for the underachiever that comes naturally. Since the underachiever knows that the law of diminishing returns applies everywhere, the joy of an occasional chocolate bar is not expected to be a long-term substitute for love or friendship. A good beer (or two) isn't meant to kill the pain of working too hard. With this in mind, a little laziness in dieting can do wonders for your health.

THE UNDERACHIEVER'S WORKOUT

Exercise has become an all-or-nothing activity. What's-the-point couch potatoes shrug off exercise to the point that they can't even walk up a flight of stairs. Overachievers train as though they're headed for the X Games. Loath to throw in with the first group, most people *think* they should cast their lot with the second, accumulating Butt Masters, Thigh Blasters, Ab Catapults, and Calf Crunchers that nobody really wants to use. Months or years down the road, they rediscover these useless items under beds and in closets like the spring-and-steel skeletons of long-neglected pets. How many people with gym memberships do you know who feel no guilt about how often they go to the gym? For every life potentially improved and extended by *modest* exercise, there's another that has been significantly impaired or shortened by the insane drive for intense physical activity.

The underachiever assumes that most people who choose to engage in extreme fitness programs probably are doing so out of some unfortunate shortcoming elsewhere in their lives. ("No pain, no gain" = no brain.) Akin to the comfort-food junkie, the intense fitness buff substitutes exercise for relationships, spiritual needs, or some other human longing. Conversely, there are those who were competitive athletes in their youth, only to find that they could make more money doing taxes than playing ball. For them, fitness is a real stumbling block; they can't stand the thought of exercising

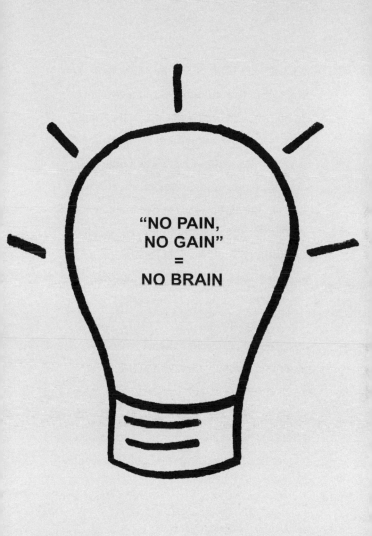

in a half-assed way. Since they don't have the time to run five miles or swim for two hours straight, they figure it's not worth the trouble. Pretty soon their bodies reflect that attitude, when all they really needed was a little slacker kind-of-do mentality to stay in shape. A walk in the morning, and maybe five minutes with weights in the evening, and they'd have all the fitness they'd need for a lifetime. Skipping workouts isn't a problem for the underachiever, either, since that presents the perfect opportunity to rest. After all, if you work out all the time, you'll never have a chance to discover how good it feels when you take a break.

For those who are just starting on their path to modest fitness, going to the gym, hiring a trainer, and reading a bunch of books by intense fitness gurus will probably just lead to frustration: it's pretty demoralizing to surround yourself with people who make you look bad by comparison. And when the improvements don't come fast enough (they never do), odds are you'll just cash it in anyway. Then you'll be right back where you started, but with more disappointment and a lot less money.

What follows is the couldn't-be-easier Underachiever's Workout:

1. Walk.
2. Do something with your upper body. It could be push-ups, or light weights, or gardening.
3. If you feel like it, do a little stretching before bed. I'm not talking yoga here. Simply relax and unknot those muscles that could use a little loosening.

4. Sleep a lot. Studies have shown that getting plenty of rest can really improve your results when it comes to losing weight.

There, don't you feel better already?

THE UNDERACHIEVER'S FINANCIAL PLAN

The underachiever is primed for financial success. Sure, money's great, and lots of it would be nice, but is it worth the soul-killing burnout hours necessary to get it? The hard work of the ascetic who saves through deprivation isn't worth the trouble, either. Luckily, there is a middle path. Rest assured, underachievement will do wonders for your bank account.

The underachiever can't help but notice that there are a lot of people who have lost their shirts looking for a big payoff in the stock market. Not content with average market returns, the overachiever strives to find the hot stock. But that's what everyone's looking for. When there's a whiff of fast money in the air, investors pile on and hope to get in and out before the assumed collapse, ahead of the other overachievers hoping to do the same thing. It's this sort of mad, high-stakes chase that leads to the overvalued market bubbles that burst and clean everybody out.

As it turns out, the finding and the bailing out aren't so easy to do. Index funds are typically more successful than those that are actively managed, and the underachiever reasons (correctly) that if highly skilled, even brilliant, fund managers can't beat the market, then it's pretty unlikely that he will, either.

More important, the underachiever doesn't let mania for competitive achievement get in the way of good results. It's simply true that human optimism (and greed) are the primary sources of wealth for Vegas casinos and corporations with a knack for creative accounting. And if international accounting and banking firms are sometimes fooled by clever CFOs, then it's a good bet that you will be, too. For every stock pick that looks prescient in hindsight, there are probably five other picks that went nowhere but down.

Consider all the financially overextended overachievers desperate for the big win who are especially vulnerable to market downturns. They like holding on to overpriced stocks long after they should have sold for a comfortable gain, all in the interest of stretching a good gain into a phenomenal one. In the end, they wind up losing everything.

The underachiever doesn't have to invest to impress: she's already saving a bundle of money by living the underachiever's way. She doesn't drive the most expensive car, buy the fanciest clothes, or pay for the expensive personal trainer to get into perfect condition. This leaves more money to invest, and it doesn't pressure her into overreaching with her portfolio.

The key is the wealth ratio:

$$\frac{\text{What you HAVE}}{\text{What you WANT}}$$

If what you want is modest, what you have is greater by comparison.

Enjoy the peace of mind that comes with investing the underachiever's way. Index funds and IRAs are a lot easier to deal with than speculative real estate ventures and the scramble for "growth stocks." By avoiding the temptation of huge gains, you'll enjoy the safety that comes from avoiding huge losses. You won't get to brag about it; you'll just have to be happy with all that extra money.

THE UNDERACHIEVER
AT HOME

The family that underachieves together stays together. That should be evident by now, since it is clear that underachievement (1) promotes healthier, more durable relationships; (2) leaves more time to enjoy a variety of activities; and (3) saves money. All that can add up to a felicitous environment for rearing happy, healthy, underachieving children.

This is not to suggest that you don't care about your children's future. Just don't go nuts trying to turn them into the next Mozart by age three, or worse, stress out about their achievements before they even leave the womb. (Take comfort in the fact that Mozart learned how to play the piano pretty well without benefit of "Baby Mozart" videos or in utero training.) Too many Little League parents and soccer moms push and cajole their kids as if they're going to turn the kids pro. It can be addicting to see "mini-you" kicking the crap out of the competition, whatever the activity, but it's a recipe for disaster. We've seen what the overachieving winner mentality brings: the inevitability of dashed hopes, resentment, therapy, and the eventual tell-all, score-settling memoir. It's also a time-honored, hardwired tradition for children to not want what their parents push on them. The more intense the achievement campaign, the more likely and stronger the backlash.

In contrast, the underachieving parent finds the balance that leads to family harmony. He doesn't push himself too hard, so he doesn't feel

THE FAMILY THAT
UNDERACHIEVES
TOGETHER
STAYS
TOGETHER

the need to drive his family insane, either. He has time to enjoy his kids when he's not tired and stressed out. And the underachieving parent has the kind of contentment that keeps him from passing on frustrated dreams to kids who are busy enough trying to live their own lives. The underachieving parent doesn't succumb to the temptation of turning children into status symbols. Your happy memories of childhood? Probably not high-stress sports activities or piano drills. The difference between a happy and an unhappy childhood is the difference between encouragement and pressure.

In fact, when it comes to creating families, overachievers are hopelessly outmatched by their relatively lazy counterparts. Overachievers never find the "right time" to settle down. If they don't psych themselves out of parenthood completely, they squeeze it in and then feel compromised.

Underachievers don't plan to worry parenting down to the last detail, so it's not so intimidating. They have no idea how much money they'll spend on diapers, they didn't plan on music lessons, and they probably forgot that small people don't always sleep soundly. Perhaps they didn't realize until junior moved in how cramped a two-bedroom apartment could be. In any event, they just muddle through it one day at a time, which in the humbling and beautiful world of having kids is about all you can ask for.

THE UNDERACHIEVER'S FAITH: TRUE ENLIGHTEN-MENT

Would that underachievement were its own religion, holding as it does the keys to contentment, happiness, and a well-balanced life.

Religion is too often the pretext for war, hatred, intolerance among different faiths, and competitive piety within faiths. But the problem isn't with faith, or even with difference in faith, within the churches, synagogues, temples, and mosques. The problem is the overachievers in those institutions.

When people feel the need to prove themselves more worthy than their neighbors, that's when the trouble starts. It can happen within a church, when some members are absolutely convinced that God prefers one sort of recognition over another. Or it can happen when members of a particular faith decide that the rest of the world needs to see things their way, and their way only. For too many people, faith becomes another means of achievement. Instead of striving for the worldly successes of money or fame, the religious overachiever competes for special cosmic significance or special favor with God. To believe that you are God's only gift to the world puts you at odds with the six billion other people who might like to feel the same way. If the faith of underachievement holds anything to be true, it's that by not striving to be better than someone else, you're free to better yourself.

THE RESULTS SPEAK FOR THEMSELVES

OVERACHIEVEMENT

frustration

angry colleagues

knee surgery

traffic jams

isolation

extremism

stock market crashes

heart disease

depression

UNDERACHIEVEMENT

serenity

peaceful work relations

moderate fitness

smooth commutes

friendship

humble faith

sustainable economic growth

low blood pressure

contentment

A HELPFUL QUIZ

The following questions are designed to make sure that you've learned just enough—and not one bit more than necessary—to begin underachieving *today*. Instructions for scoring your exam are provided, with your total score serving as your Underachiever's Quotient, or "U.Q."

1. Your boss asks you to complete a set of forms to satisfy an inspector. You should:
   a. Be sure you use the correct font.
   b. Create the forms from scratch.
   c. Crib from last year's forms.
   d. Enlist the help of colleagues, and together stall for time.

2. You decide to embark upon a fitness program. Choose from among the following options:
   a. Investigate local triathlons.
   b. Hire a personal trainer.
   c. Start walking around your neighborhood each day.
   d. Buy a home gym device shaped like a medieval catapult.

3.   You're out on a date . . .

     . . . well, that's enough, isn't it? Good for
you! Life's full of tests. Let's just not, shall we?
     By the way, if you're disappointed that
you didn't get to determine your personal U.Q.,
then you've just flunked.

CONCLUSION

By now, you should be completely confident that underachievement is the key to happiness in your life, and for everyone else around you. Stop worrying about not being perfect. Dedicate yourself to the pleasures and benefits of mediocrity.

As Aristotle once said, the mark of an educated individual is to demand no more precision from a subject than the subject itself allows. That seems to apply, doesn't it?

Remember, underachievement isn't about doing absolutely *nothing.* It's about the *right effort* at the *right time,* in the *right place.* And not one bit more.

So go ahead and start living life to the minimum. Consider the areas in which you're striving for success against your own best interests. Don't take any so-called achievement seriously.

And now that you've seen the light, turn it off. You're wasting valuable energy. Because you're already good enough.

You must always work not just within, but below your means. If you can handle three elements, handle only two. If you can handle ten, then handle only five. In that way, the ones you do handle, you handle with more ease, more mastery, and you create a feeling of strength in reserve.

—Pablo Picasso

ABOUT THE AUTHOR

Ray Bennett is a medical specialist in Seattle and a recovering overachiever. He is still guilty of overachievement in the care of his patients, however, and he lives with his wife and children among too many overachieving neighbors.

SOME BLANK PAGES

THE UNDERACHIEVER'S MANIFESTO

THE UNDERACHIEVER'S MANIFESTO

THE UNDERACHIEVER'S MANIFESTO

Good enough